★ ★ ★ ★ ★ ★ ★ ★ ★ ★ ★ ★ ★ ★

ANNUAL CARNIVAL
NEXT SATURDAY

Coming to town! Rides,
Games, Food, and more!

1

The most exciting and huge thing will happen tomorrow, and Sarah and Yusuf can't wait. The carnival that comes every year to the town is one of Sarah and Yusuf's favorite places.

The sister and brother have fun all day sitting on rides and playing games with their friends. Last year, Yusuf won a huge stuffed bear that was bigger than himself!

"Come on, Yusuf! You're making us all late!" yelled Sarah the next morning.

The day of the carnival was here, and Yusuf was making his older sister mad by taking forever to get ready.

5

Once the family was ready, they drove to the carnival. In the car, Yusuf looked out the window and could already spot a tall roller coaster that became bigger as they came nearer.

Once they jumped out of the car, Sarah and Yusuf ran inside the carnival.
"I think I'll go on that ride first," said Sarah, pointing to the spinning teacups.

"We need to get tickets first!" reminded Yusuf. Once they got their tickets and bought some lemonade, Yusuf and Sarah got in line for the teacups.

"Wow," said Yusuf, drinking his lemonade, "this line is so long!"
And it *was* very long. About fifteen people were waiting to go on the ride.
"I'm not waiting this long!" exclaimed Yusuf, his lemonade flying out of his hand. He gasped as he watched it spill all over the boy standing in front of them.

"Yusuf!" Sarah yelled. "Look what you did!"
Yusuf's face reddened. He looked up and found a sour-faced man and an angry boy.

11

"Of course," the man said, crossing his arms. "YOUR kind causing destruction everywhere." Yusuf's eyes turned wide. This man clearly thought Muslims were bad.

"S-sorry," Yusuf mumbled, his voice quivering. The man's cold eyes seemed to freeze Yusuf and Sarah to their spots.

"Excuse me, sir," Sarah said sweetly with a smile. "Islam is a very peaceful religion, and we're very sorry about the lemonade. My brother wasn't paying attention."

What was Sarah doing? Talking to a man who clearly didn't like them? But Yusuf reminded himself that Sarah never wanted anyone to be mad at her. She always talked to the person and tried explaining to them.

15

The man turned to Sarah curiously.
"Oh, really?" he asked. "Peaceful?"
Sarah nodded happily. "Yes, and if you want, I can tell you all about Islam."
The man's thin mouth curved into a mocking smirk. "Alright. Tell me everything you've got."

YUSUF

SARA

MR. MILLER

JACK

"Allow me to introduce myself first. I'm Sarah," Sarah explained, pointing to herself. "And that's my brother Yusuf."

The man's cold expression didn't change at all. "Mr. Miller." he said. "Jack," he said again, tilting his head slightly towards the young boy. So the man was Mr. Miller, Yusuf told himself, and the boy who he dropped lemonade on was Jack.

The boy, Jack, looked at Yusuf. "You look my age. What's your name?"

"Yusuf. Nice to meet you, Jack and Mr. Miller. And I'm really sorry about spilling that all over you."

"Nah, it's fine," said Jack. Sarah, Yusuf, Jack and his dad, Mr. Miller, all moved forward in the line. It was almost their turn.

"Okay, Mr. Miller. Let's begin," Sarah said. Before she could say another word, Yusuf exclaimed, "Sarah, we don't have much time! It's our turn after this." Looking ahead, they could see that their turn was coming soon.

But Sarah didn't look worried at all. "I remember this one method of sharing Islam that I heard from a lecture. It covers the main points of Islam in only three minutes or less! It's very easy and very simple to remember." she said.

Yusuf's eyes widened. How could her sister explain all of Islam in less than five minutes?

"OMG-HI!" Sarah said with a grin.

"What?"

"Omg-hi. Here, let me explain. Each letter stands for something." Sarah began.

She turned to Mr. Miller and said. "We believe in one God, who we call Allah, and we believe he has no partners, sons or daughters, or mother and father. He is all Merciful and all Hearing and all Knowing."

Mr. Miller raised an eyebrow and took a step closer, but his expression was still just as cold.

Sarah turned back to Yusuf, "See, that was the first letter. 'O,' for One God."

M =
Messengers

"Then we believe in Messengers," Sarah told Mr. Miller, "to help humans, God chose certain people to spread the message of one God and His guidance. They are called messengers. Some of them were Moses, Jesus, and Abraham."

YUSUF

27

"Hey, and don't forget Yusuf!" interrupted Yusuf. Sarah laughed. "Yes, and my brother was named after one Messenger. You may be familiar with the name Joseph. But Muslims call it Yusuf. It's the same thing."
"Yes, we know Joseph. That's why your brother's name sounded so familiar." said Mr. Miller.

Jack smiled at Yusuf. "That's so cool. You were named after Joseph, a Messenger."
"Ya, it is cool," said Yusuf. "I love my name."
Then he realized something. "Wait, Sarah. The letter 'M' stands for Messengers, right?"

G =
GUIDANCE

Sarah nodded. "And now 'G' for guidance. The Quran is our holy book that was given from God to Prophet Muhammed, peace be upon him, our last Messenger, as a guidance for all of humanity."

"You know, Mr. Miller," continued Sarah, "Just like we're following the rules of this carnival, like we can't skip the lines or throw garbage on the ground, so we all have a better experience, in the same way, we believe that God has given rules for us to follow to have peace in this world."
Yusuf's face lit up. "Ya, and we follow the rules to go to Jannah!"

31

"Jannah?" asked Jack confusingly, his face lighting up. "Is that like a theme park or something?" Yusuf laughed while Sarah smiled politely. "No, but it's waaay better than any theme park. Anything's possible there."

"Whoa!" exclaimed Jack.

"It's the place we go after we die if we were good in this world," Yusuf told him, still laughing about what Jack said.

CO-WORKERS

Mr. Miller nodded. "I have some Muslim co-workers at work, and I think I've heard of that word before. They also read the Quran during their break time. It sounds... well, it's unlike anything I've ever heard."

"It really is special," agrees Sarah.
Mr. Miller seemed interested now about Islam.
"Sarah, we finished O-M-G, right? Now it's 'H', for Hajj?" Yusuf guessed.

"That's a good guess, but no, 'H' stands for-"
Sarah was interrupted by Yusuf tugging on her skirt.
"What?!" she yelled angrily.
Yusuf was pointing to the ride. The teacups were
slowing down and people were getting ready to get off
the ride, laughing and unbuckling seat belts.
"It's our turn!"
Sarah waved her hand dismissively. "I will finish in time,
this doesn't take long."

H = HEREAFTER

She turned back to Mr. Miller and Jack. "So Jack, when you follow your teacher, you get a good grade, right?"

Jack nodded slowly. "Yeah."

"Likewise," continued Sarah, "we believe that our teacher is God and He will give us a very good prize, Jannah. So we believe that after we die, God will bring us back to life and God will judge us. He will ask us, 'Did you follow my guidance and instructions?' If we did, God, by his mercy, will put us in Jannah, paradise."

"Interesting," said a voice behind them.
Sarah and Yusuf whirled around and faced a short lady with a bright purple sweater. It was strange because it was such a hot summer day. Next to her were two other ladies with long black hair holding hands with three kids, All the ladies were in line and leaning in towards Sarah. They seemed to be listening to the conversation too.
Yusuf was amazed how Sarah was teaching so many people at once about Islam. She didn't even know these people, and yet they were still interested.
Sarah, now aware that more people were listening, spoke a little louder over the noises of music and talking coming from the carnival.
"Mr. Miller, what do you think about everything I've just said?"

The gate opened and Sarah, Yusuf, Jack, Mr. Miller, and the ladies behind them all began searching for a teacup to sit in. The brother and sister walked towards a huge blue one and Jack and his dad rushed towards a yellow one.

"You know what, let me think about it for a while, "Mr. Miller shouted across to the teacup where Sarah and Yusuf were seated. The teacups began to twirl slowly. Sarah and Yusuf twisted the handle as hard as they could to make their teacup spin the fastest. Yusuf crushed Sarah and the other way around as they rotated at top speed, barely hearing their own screams and laughter over the rushing wind and the carnival that was now a blur of colors around them. Too soon, the teacups reached a halt, and Yusuf was disappointed that the ride was over.

"THAT WAS AMAZING!" he yelled. He caught Jack's eye in the yellow teacup and they both shared a wide grin. Everyone got off and walked towards the exit. Mr. Miller and Jack caught up with Sarah and Yusuf.

"On the ride, I was thinking hard about what you explained for me." Jack's dad told Sarah and Yusuf. "And I think... It all make sense!"
Sarah couldn't hide her happiness and hugged Yusuf tightly. Yusuf's mouth hung wide open as his sister broke the hug.

Could Mr. Miller actually become a Muslim-hater to a Muslim-lover all because of two kids?
"I clearly knew very little about Islam. I thought all you Muslims were bad people! If you hadn't explained your religion to me, I would have continued to think like that. Do you mind taking me to meet your parents?" said Mr. Miller. "I'd like to speak to them about their amazing kids!"
Sarah and Yusuf ran to their parents, Jack and Mr. Miller following close behind.

"Mama, Abbu, this man wants to speak with you"
Their parents stood up from the bench and looked at Mr. Miller. "Hello," said Yusuf's mom, looking confused.
Mr. Miller waved a hand. "Hi, I'm Liam Miller. I just wanted to tell you that you have such smart, great kids! They've explained all about Islam in only three minutes as we were waiting in line. They speak like they're professors on the topic or something!"

Yusuf's parents glanced at their kids. "Oh really?" said Yusuf's dad.
"Yes! where do they learn all of this?" Mr. Miller asked.
Yusuf's parents, still surprised by what Mr. Miller said about their kids explaining Islam to a non-Muslim, told Mr. Miller that they learned at their Islamic school and all the lectures they listened to about sharing Islam.

"I really think your religion makes a lot of sense. All the ideas seem to fit together like in a puzzle." "Would you like to learn more?" asked Yusuf's dad pulling out his phone. "We'd be happy to explain further. I'll give you my phone number." "Absolutely!" said Mr. Miller enthusiastically.

After they exchanged phone numbers, they made a plan to meet up at the local mosque so that more Muslims there can talk with Mr. Miller, so that maybe, one day, he will become Muslim too.

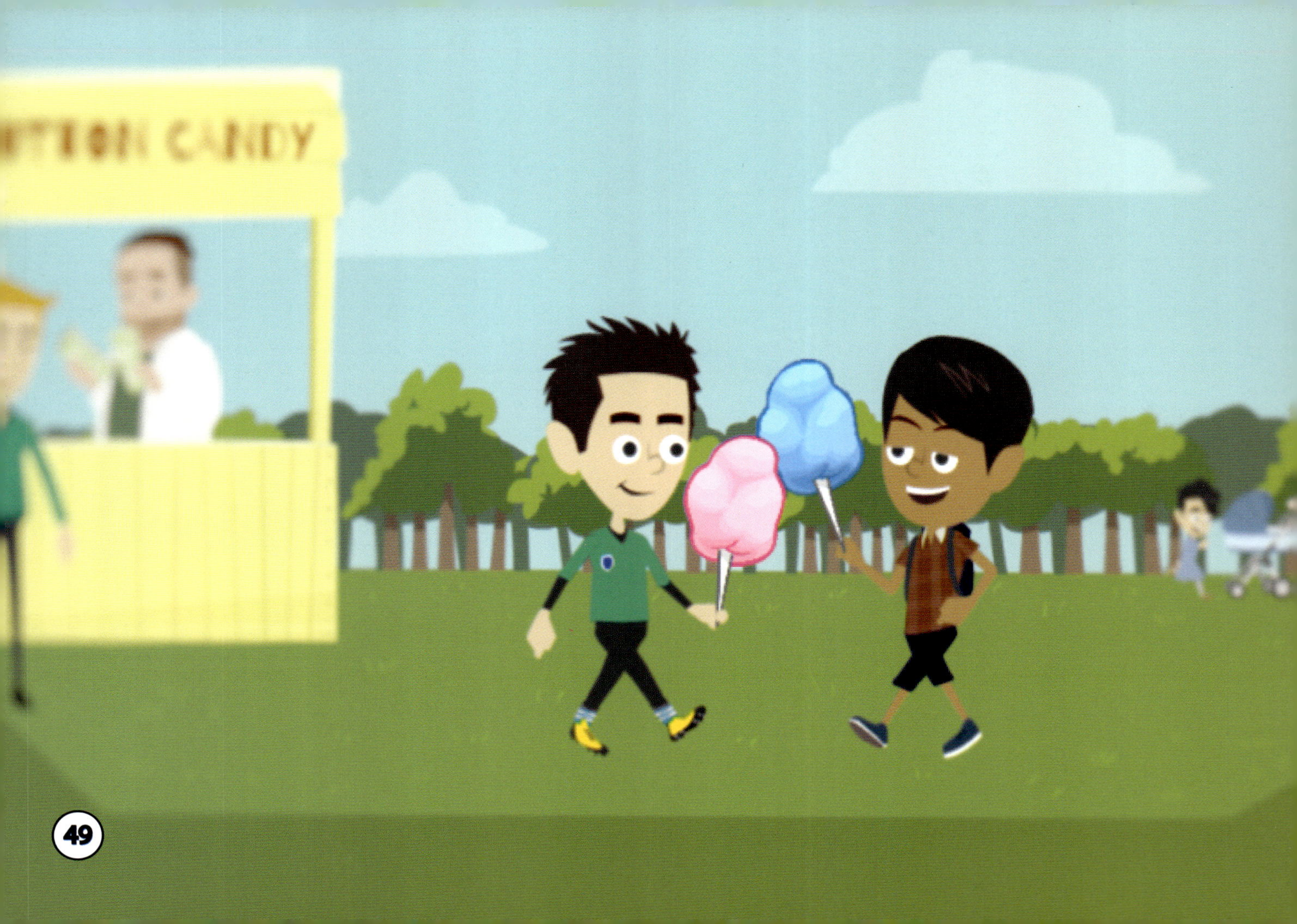
CANDY

The rest of the day was filled with endless fun and a lot of cotton candy. Jack and Yusuf found more things they liked in common, like their favorite video games and sports, and became good friends as they played games and sat on more rides for the rest of the afternoon.

Yusuf even won another huge stuffed bear, an exact copy of the one he won last year.

Even the lady with the purple sweater and other ladies that were behind them in the teacup line found Sarah and Yusuf and thanked them for teaching them more about Islam.

They said they would read more books on it because they heard wrong things on TV and on the news about Islam, but now that Sarah and Yusuf told them the truth about their religion, they wanted to clear those doubts.

I = INVITATION

A while later, Yusuf suddenly realized something. "Sarah, in O-M-G-H-I, you never told me what 'I' stood for."
"Oh Yeah," she said. " 'I' was what we did just now. 'I' stood for 'Invitation'. We invited Mr. Miller and those ladies to learn more about Islam and maybe even become Muslims."

"Oh," understood Yusuf, "I get it now."
The afternoon turned into evening, and it was time for both Jack's and Yusuf's families to leave the carnival and go home.

O ONE GOD

M MESSENGERS

G GUIDANCE

H HEREAFTER

I INVITATION